Tiger Talk
People I Know

Mum and Dad

Leon Read

W
FRANKLIN WATTS
LONDON • SYDNEY

Contents

Look out for Tiger on the pages of this book. Sometimes he is hiding.

Mums and dads are part of a family.

Every family is different.

Different families

Mums and dads are different too!

My dad is good at drawing.

Our dad is cool!

4

My mummy
has black hair.

My mum
loves
cuddles.

Jacob used a camera
to take pictures of
his mum and dad.

5

Having fun

Belonging to a family is fun.

Kira's dad gives her a piggy back.

I am flying!

We are having a picnic.

How do you have fun with your family?

7

Animal families

Shaz and Tiger are playing
with a family of chimps.

Now the chimps
are hiding from
Tiger!

Lions

Elephants

Geese

What other animal
families can you
think of?

9

Teaching us

Mums and dads
teach us lots
of things.

From letters,

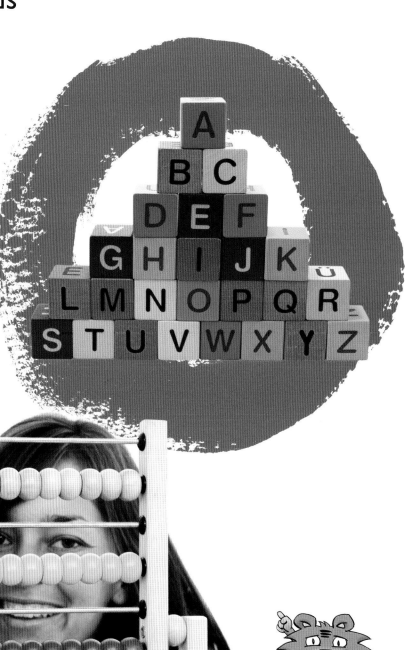

to counting.

10

From how
to behave,

to how to
play games.

My dad
taught me to
play Snap.

Things I like...

There are special things we like to do with our mum and dad.

I like reading with my daddy.

12

I like going to the playground with Mummy.

I like playing football with my dad.

What special things do you like to do?

Fe_ling bett_r

Mums and dads
help us to feel better.

Dad cheers up Carmel.

Harry's
mum makes
him laugh.

14

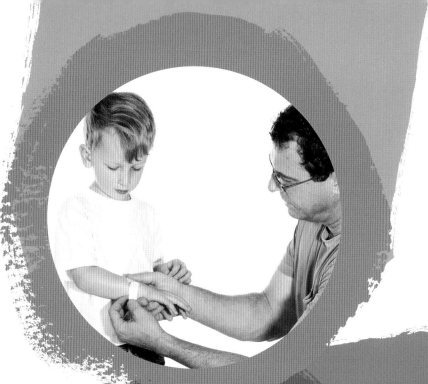

Peter's dad
gives him
a plaster.

Emma is ill.
Her mum
looks after
her.

When was the last
time you felt ill
or upset?

Going to work

Many mums and dads go out to work to earn money.

Some people work inside.

Some people work outside.

What job do you want to do when you grow up?

Real names

Mums and dads have
real names, just like us.

My daddy's
name is Michael.

Riaz

Gemma

Sarah

Sunny

Most people have a middle name too.

My middle name is Clive.

What is your middle name?

19

Playing House

Mica likes playing pretend families with Freddie.

Mum is looking after baby.

It is fun playing families.

Daddy is cooking dinner.

21

Me and my family

Shaz is drawing a picture of her family.

I am drawing
my mummy first.

It is fun playing families.

Daddy is cooking dinner.

21

Me and my family

Shaz is drawing a picture of her family.

I am drawing my mummy first.

Draw a picture of your family.

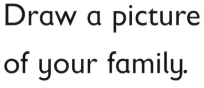

Who are the important people in your life?

Word picture bank

cuddles – P. 5

ill – P. 15

letters – P. 10

piggy back – P. 6

playground – P. 13

snap – P. 11

First published in 2008 by Franklin Watts
338 Euston Road, London NW1 3BH

Franklin Watts Australia
Level 17/207 Kent Street, Sydney NSW 2000

Copyright © Franklin Watts 2008

Series editor: Adrian Cole
Photographer: Andy Crawford (unless otherwise credited)
Design: Sphere Design Associates
Art director: Jonathan Hair
Consultants: Prue Goodwin and Karina Law

A CIP catalogue record for this book is available
from the British Library.

ISBN: 978 0 7496 8110 4

Dewey Classification: 306.874

Acknowledgements:
The Publisher would like to thank Norrie Carr model agency. 'Tiger' puppet used
with kind permission from Ravensden PLC (www.ravensden.co.uk). Tiger Talk logo
drawn by Kevin Hopgood. Photo credits: cover Patricia Marks/Shutterstock. 1, 3bl, 6r,
19b, 24bl Edyta Pawlowska/ Shutterstock. 3t HTuller/Shutterstock. 3br Olga Lyubkina/
Shutterstock. 4t Yuri Arcurs/Shutterstock. 4b, 11b, 24br Karen Struthers/ Shutterstock.
5t, 12 digitalskillet/Shutterstock. 5c, 24tl Anna Chelnokova/Shutterstock. 5b, 6l
Losevsky Pavel/Shutterstock. 7t, 19t Glenda M. Powers/Shutterstock. 7b iofoto/
Shutterstock. 9l Kristian Sekulic/Shutterstock. 9c Norma Cornes/Shutterstock. 9r Jeff
Thrower (WebThrower)/ Shutterstock. 10t, 24tr Elena Schweitzer/Shutterstock. 10b
Matka Wariatka/Shutterstock. p 11t Tomasz Trojanowski/Shutterstock. 13t, 24bc Fei
Dongliang/Shutterstock. 13b Elena Elisseeva/Shutterstock. 14t 2734725246/
Shutterstock. 14b Jaimie Duplass/Shutterstock. 15t Bettina Baumgartner/Shutterstock.
15b, 24tc Jamie Wilson/Shutterstock. 16 Radu Razvan/Shutterstock. 17t+b Stephen
Coburn/Shutterstock. 18 Jason Stitt/Shutterstock.

Every attempt has been made to clear copyright. Should there be any
inadvertent omission please apply to the publisher for rectification.

Printed in China

Franklin Watts is a division
of Hachette Children's Books,
an Hachette Livre UK company.

There are 18 Tigers, including me, in this book.
Did you find all of us?